MASKS

Ting and Neil Morris

Illustrated by Ruth Levy

SEA-TO-SEA
Mankato Collingwood London

 This symbol appears on some pages throughout this book. It indicates that adult supervision is advisable for that activity.

This edition first published in 2007 by
Sea-to-Sea Publications
1980 Lookout Drive
North Mankato
Minnesota 56003

Printed in China

Library of Congress Cataloging in Publication Data

Morris, Ting.
    Masks / by Ting and Neil Morris (authors) ; Ruth Levy (illustrator).
        p. cm. -- (Sticky fingers)
    Includes bibliographical references and index.
    ISBN   *978-1-59771-030-5
    1. Mask making--Juvenile literature. 2. Masks--Juvenile literature. I. Morris, Neil,
1946- II. Levy, Ruth. III. Title.

TT898.M49 2006
646.4'78-dc22

                                                                    2005058153

9 8 7 6 5 4 3 2

Published by arrangement with the Watts Publishing Group Ltd, London

Editor: Hazel Poole
Designer: Sally Boothroyd
Photography: John Butcher
Artwork: Ruth Levy
Models: Emma Morris
Picture research: Ambreen Husain/Joanne King

Contents

Introduction

In this book you can learn about masks both by reading about them and by having fun with craft activities. The information in the fact boxes will tell you about masks from all over the world - their history, why and how they were made, how they were used, and what they were made of. Of course, many types of mask are still in use today and you will learn about these too. Did you know that clowns painted their faces on eggs? You can read about this and see how to paint your own egg faces.

At the end of the book is a world map to show you where all the masks come from. There is also a list of places to visit and books to read if you want to find out more.

So get ready to get your fingers sticky - making masks as you read about them!

Equipment and materials

The projects in this book provide an introduction to the use of different art and craft media, and need little adult help. Most of the objects are made with throwaway household "junk" such as boxes, plastic bottles and containers, newspaper, and fabric remnants. Natural things such as seeds, sticks, sand, and stones are also used. Paints, brushes, glues, and modeling materials will have to be bought, but if stored correctly will last for a long time and for many more craft activities.

In this book the following materials are used:

air-hardening modeling clay
balloons (round)
beads
brushes (for glue and paint)
buttons
cardboard boxes
cardboard tubes
cellophane
cloth
clothespins
cooking oil
curtain fabric
dowel rods (wooden)
egg cartons
eggshells
elastic
felt scraps
felt-tip pens
flour
fork
Fun Tak
glue (water-based PVA, which can be used for thickening paint and as a varnish; strong glue such as UHU for sticking plastic, metal, and fabric; glue stick)
jar (for mixing paint and paste)
knife (blunt)
oak tag

paint (powder, ready-mixed or poster paints; gold paint)
paper (thick construction paper; brown craft paper; crêpe paper; tissue paper; newspaper)
paper bags
paper doilies
paper plates
pencils (including white)
pin (straight)
popsicle stick
rolling pin
ruler
salt
scissors
sequins
silver foil
sponge
stapler
sticks
straws
string
tape (parcel tape; masking tape; foil tape) and adhesive-backed pads
trays and tubs
varnish (PVA mixed with cold water)
Vaseline
wallpaper paste (fungicide-free)
water
yarn

Pharaoh's Golden Mask

Go back in time to the mysterious world of ancient Egypt with this papier-mâché mask.

MESSY ACTIVITY

You will need to cover your work surface before you begin.

YOU WILL NEED:
- ✔round balloon ✔fungicide-free wallpaper paste ✔pencil
- ✔scissors or craft knife ✔newspaper ✔masking tape
- ✔red and yellow oak tag ✔PVA glue ✔poster paints ✔pin
- ✔stapler ✔bowl ✔thin cardboard ✔Vaseline ✔water
- ✔gold paint (bought in powder form and mixed with PVA)

1 Blow up a balloon to a size a bit bigger than your head, and coat it with Vaseline. To hold it steady while you are working, put the balloon in an empty bowl. Now tear up some old newspaper into strips about 1 in (3 cm) wide.

2 Mix the wallpaper paste as instructed on the package, and coat the strips of newspaper with it. Pull each strip between your finger and thumb to remove any lumps before sticking them onto the balloon. Cover the balloon with at least five layers of paste-coated paper. Leave it to dry–which might take three or four days!

3 When the mask is dry, burst the balloon with a pin. Ask an adult to help cut a deep hollow in the back. Fit the mask over your head and ask an adult to mark the position of your eyes. Take the mask off so that the adult can cut eyeholes and a breathing hole.

4 For the nose, fold a piece of cardboard as shown. Tape the nose around the breathing hole with masking tape.

5 Paint the mask with gold paint. When it is dry, complete the pharaoh's makeup by outlining the eyes with black and blue poster paint and adding red lips.

6 You could also make a pharaoh's crown. Cut out this shape from red oak tag, making it big enough to fit around your head when you are wearing the mask. Staple the ends together.

7 Cut out a cobra's head from yellow oak tag and glue it on the front of the crown. This is what the crown of Lower Egypt looked like. Now put on your mask and crown to be an Egyptian pharaoh.

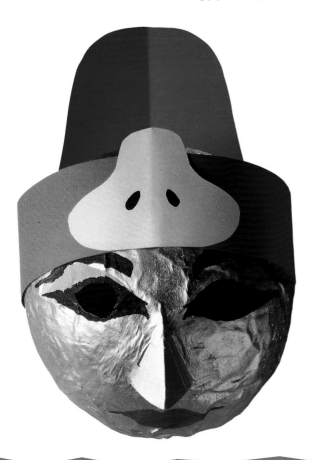

Tutankhamen

In ancient Egypt the king, or pharaoh, was treated as a god. Tutankhamen was a boy-king. He was only about nine years old when he became king in about 1347 B.C. He died before he was 20, and his body was preserved as a mummy. His funeral took place in the Valley of the Kings, a burial center near the ancient city of Thebes. When Tutankhamen's tomb was later discovered in 1922, it was found to be filled with over 5,000 precious objects–thrones, chariots, swords, statues, rings, and even toys. The boy-king's coffin had been closed for over 3,200 years. A solid gold mask covered the head and shoulders of his mummified body. The master craftsman of the time must have created this mask, for no one else would have been allowed to model the sacred face of the pharaoh.

On Stage

1 To make the stage, cut the top and flaps off a cardboard box, and then cut away one side of the box.

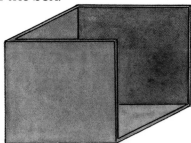

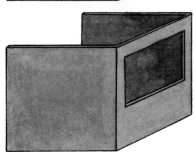

2 For the front of the stage, cut a window in the other side of the box. Cover the box with colored paper and add decorations.

YOU WILL NEED:
✓ large cardboard box   ✓ paper doily
✓ colored construction paper   ✓ oak tag
✓ 2 big buttons   ✓ PVA glue   ✓ string
✓ 2 clothespins   ✓ 6 paper bags   ✓ water
✓ 3 cardboard tubes   ✓ glue brush
✓ masking tape   ✓ elastic   ✓ poster paint
✓ fabric   ✓ silver foil   ✓ felt-tip pens
✓ scissors   ✓ straws   ✓ tissue paper

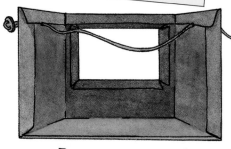

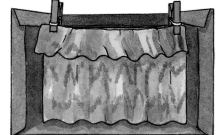

3 Make a small hole in each side near the top of the box. Tie a button to one end of a piece of string and thread the string through the two holes. Pull the string tight and tie the second button to the other end. Hang the fabric curtain over the string and hold it in place with clothespins.

4 Make three Japanese *No* actors and masks for them to wear on stage. Put one paper bag inside another and fill it with crumpled-up newspaper. Push a cardboard tube into the bag and fasten the neck with masking tape.

5 Flatten the pointed corners and tape them down with masking tape. Make two more paper-bag heads in the same way.

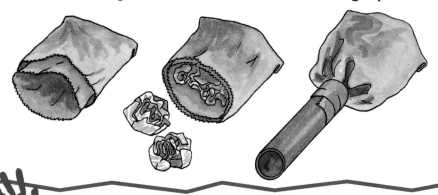

6 For the masks, cut out three ovals from oak tag. Make them slightly bigger than the paper-bag heads. Paint and decorate the masks—one the face of a woman, another a man, and the third a demon. The woman's hair can be made of painted paper doily decorated with tissue-paper flowers. The man has green bead eyes and straws for hair. Cut the demon out of red oak tag. Glue on scrunched-up silver-foil horns and eyes.

7 Finally, make two small holes in the masks. Thread some elastic through the holes. Now you can put the masks on the Japanese *No* actors and let the performance begin.

Ancient Japanese theater

No is an ancient form of Japanese theater that developed in the fourteenth century. The word "no" means "talent" or "skill." *No* performers are all men, who tell stories rather than acting them out. They wear beautifully carved wooden masks and traditional costumes. There are at least 125 types of masks including old person, man, woman, god or goddess, and demon or goblin. The carved wood is coated with plaster and then lacquered. Not very much happens in a *No* drama. The audience usually knows the plot very well, and about 230 different plays are still performed in Japan. The words are read as poetry, not sung, but chanted. The performers dance as though in a slow-motion film.

Masked Ball

1 First make a paper pattern. Fold the paper once and then copy this outline. Draw the eyeholes at least $1/2$ in (1.5 cm) from the fold. Cut out the mask and hold it to your face to see if it fits. *(This mask is 8 x 3 in (20 x 7 cm) wide.)*

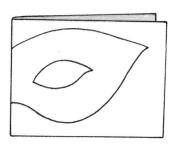

2 Put the mask on the cardboard, and hold it in position with masking tape. Draw around the shape, including the eyeholes, and cut it out.

3 Cut the frilly edge off a paper doily and tape it around the top of the mask on the back. Put a thin layer of PVA glue around the eyeholes and cover with sequins. Put more glue on top and add more sequins and beads. Cover the whole mask with glittering sequins and beads.

4 Dot some glue on a string of sequins and wind it around a stick. Tape the stick to the back of the mask.

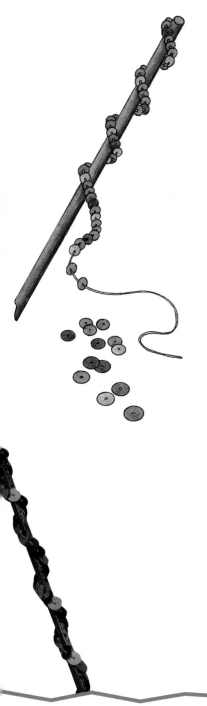

Masquerade

Guests wear masks and fancy-dress costumes to a masquerade–a party, ball, or other social gathering. Using masks in this way probably developed from Italian plays of the fourteenth century and later. These had the famous masked characters of Harlequin (below), Punchinello, and other classic figures. Usually a heavy leather mask covered all or half the player's face. Some characters wore small black masks, called halfmasks, over the upper half of their face. In later times, ballgoers copied these masks so that they could take on a new personality for an evening. Dancing was more fun because people were not sure who they were dancing with!

Finger Masks

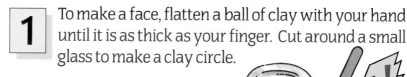

 To make a face, flatten a ball of clay with your hand until it is as thick as your finger. Cut around a small glass to make a clay circle.

2 Roll two lumps of clay into sausage-shaped tubes. To do this, roll the clay back and forth on your work surface. Make the coils long enough to fit around your circle.

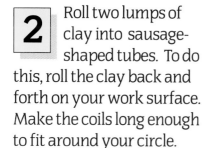

3 Moisten the edges with a damp sponge. Then stick the clay coils around the edge of the circle.

4 Use small pieces of clay to make eyes, nose, mouth, and hair.

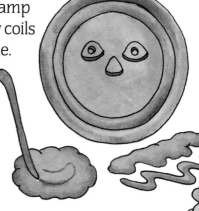

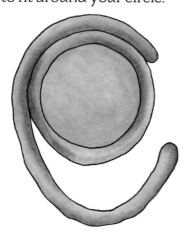

5 For the finger loops, roll a lump of clay into a coil as thick as your index finger and twice as long. Flatten the coil.

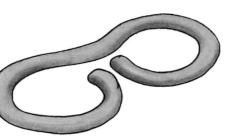

6 Shape the flattened coil into two circles, as in the picture. The circles must be big enough to fit on your fingers.

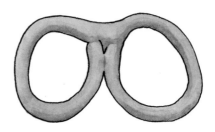

YOU WILL NEED:
- ✔ *air-hardening modeling clay*
- ✔ *blunt knife* ✔ *sponge* ✔ *varnish*
- ✔ *small glass* ✔ *poster paint*

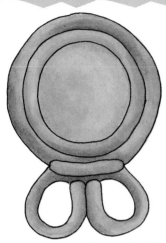

7 Moisten the bottom edge of the face and the top of the finger loops and stick them together. Strengthen the seams by pressing a thin coil of clay into them.

8 When the mask is dry, paint and varnish it. Then you could make another finger mask and act out a story.

The Inuit people

The Inuit live in the frozen Arctic regions of Alaska, Canada, Greenland, and Russia. The word Inuit means "people." Most of the 120,000 Inuit alive today live in modern houses in towns and small settlements. Previously they lived in snowhouses called igloos, skin tents, or sod houses. The dark winter days, when hunting was impossible, gave the Inuit plenty of time for singing and dancing. Men and women danced in rows, or women sometimes danced alone, waving their finger masks to act out a story. Inuit children played group games, similar to blindman's buff, and always with songs. They also played "cat's cradle," twisting a length of string around their fingers to make figures.

Thunderbird Mask Totem Pole

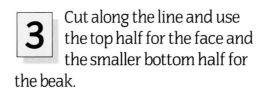

YOU WILL NEED:

- ✔ cardboard box ✔ long cardboard tube
- ✔ thick cardboard 24-27 in (60-70 cm) ✔ brushes
- ✔ colored paper ✔ brown craft paper ✔ scissors
- ✔ 3 paper plates ✔ pencil ✔ ruler ✔ glue
- ✔ egg carton cups ✔ poster paints ✔ parcel tape

1 Secure the long tube in a cardboard box. To do this, seal the box with parcel tape and cover it with brown craft paper. Cut a cross in the top and push the cardboard tube in. Paint the box with Indian symbols.

2 Now make three bird masks to go on the totem pole. Copy this basic pattern for all three birds. Fold a paper plate in half. Hold the plate upright and draw a line on it as in the picture.

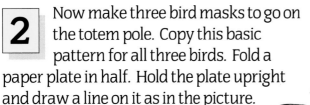

3 Cut along the line and use the top half for the face and the smaller bottom half for the beak.

4 Paint the face and beak with Indian markings. Use painted egg carton cups for eyes.

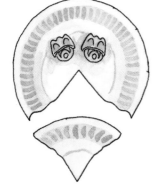

People of the totem

The tribes of the Northwest Pacific coast of America, such as the Haida and Tlingit, were the people of the totem. The brightly painted cedar totem poles are possibly the largest wood carvings in the world. There were two main types of pole. One was used as a memorial to mark the grave of Indian chiefs, and the other was built into the front of their wooden houses. The poles were made up of symbols relating to a family. Totem comes from an Indian word meaning "mark of my family." The owner's personal crest was usually at the top of the pole. Only the most powerful chiefs used the thunderbird as their crest. This legendary bird lived high in the mountains. People believed that when it flapped its wings, thunder rolled and lightning flashed.

5 To attach the beak, fold the bottom half of the plate in half and fold the ends forward. Open the beak slightly and glue the folded ends to each side of the opening.

6 For the two big thunderbird wings, cut a strip of cardboard measuring 20 x 6 in (50 x 15 cm). Decorate the strip and then cover with feather-shaped pieces of paper. Then glue it to the back of the plate.

7 Cut out a crest from colored paper and stick it on top of the thunderbird's head.

8 Use parcel tape to attach the masks to the totem pole, with the thunderbird at the top.

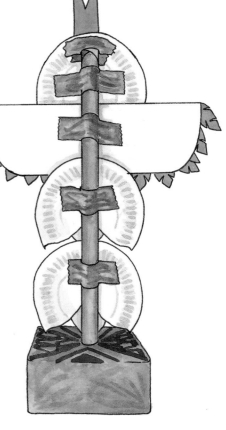

Egg Clowns

You will need to collect the empty eggshells of boiled eggs to make these funny clowns. Clean the eggshells with soapy water before you start.

1 Cut a toilet paper tube in half and cover it with colored tissue paper. Spread a little glue around the rim of the tube and put the eggshell into it. Use a white egg for a white-faced clown (or paint another egg white!), and use a brown egg for an auguste.

2 To design the face, draw the shape and size of your eggshell on paper. For a white face, the black eyebrows are important. The auguste clown has big white eyes, a red nose, and an enormous mouth. When you are happy with your design, copy the face onto the eggshell.

YOU WILL NEED:
- ✔ empty eggshells ✔ scissors
- ✔ felt-tip pens ✔ yarn ✔ glue
- ✔ paper ✔ oak tag ✔ paints
- ✔ toilet paper tube ✔ brushes
- ✔ tissue paper ✔ felt scraps

3 Draw the eyebrows, nose, and mouth with felt-tip pen. Use white paint for the auguste's eyes. Don't press too hard or your clown might crack! When the face is dry, glue on some yarn hair.

4 Make a hat for your clown. Cut a circle from felt and then cut out a piece as shown. Overlap the edges until the cone fits the egg. Glue the edges. Cut out small felt circles and glue them onto the hat. Glue the hat onto the clown's head.

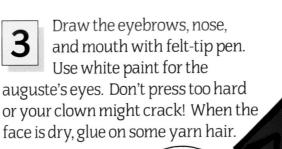

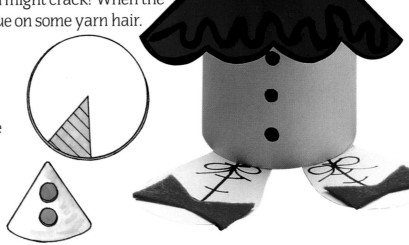

5 Copy the shapes of the bow and collar onto some oak tag. Color them in and cut them out. Then stick them to the tube bodies.

6 Clowns wear long funny shoes. Cut two long shapes from oak tag. Make some tissue paper pom-poms or felt bows and glue them to the bottom of the tube.

7 Ask an adult to help you copy your clown's makeup onto your own face using face paints.

Clowns through the ages

The first clowns date back to ancient times. In ancient Greece, bald-headed, padded buffoons appeared in plays, sometimes throwing nuts at the audience. The earliest circus clown was Joseph Grimaldi, who first appeared in England in 1781 at the age of 2! Grimaldi's clown, called Joey, did all the classic tricks—tumbling, falling over, and all forms of slapstick. One main type of clown in the circus today is known as auguste. He wears battered clothes, colorful makeup, and pretends to be very clumsy. When a clown wants to record his makeup, he paints it on an eggshell. No other clown can copy a particular makeup once it has been registered on an egg.

The traditional white-face makeup probably began with the French character of Pierrot.

African Elephant

1 First put the strong paper bag over your head to check that it fits. Then ask an adult to mark the position of your eyes. Take the bag off and cut out two small eyeholes.

YOU WILL NEED:
✓ *large paper bag, approximately 16 x 12 in (40 x 30 cm)* ✓ *pencil*
✓ *thick gray paper* ✓ *scissors* ✓ *glue*
✓ *white cardboard* ✓ *brushes*
✓ *black and white ready-mix paint*

2 Mix some black and white paint, and then paint the bag gray. Brush the paint on unevenly to make it look like wrinkled elephant's skin. When it is dry, outline the eyeholes with circles of black paint. Add more texture to the skin by painting black and white squiggly lines.

3 Cut a long strip of gray paper for the trunk. It should be wide enough to fit between the eyes and should get thinner toward the other end.

African masks

Among most African peoples, masks were an important part of their ceremonial costumes. They often wore their mask on top of the head instead of over the face. When a boy was accepted as an adult hunter, masks were worn for the ceremony. But their main purpose was to scare away evil spirits. The Bambara people of Mali had six different societies and each had its own type of mask. Some were in the form of human beings, while animal masks were decorated with real horns, quills, and feathers. The one pictured here is an antelope mask. Some masks were used in ceremonies to try and make rain fall. The Idoma people of Nigeria had many dance societies. These societies had special masks for hunters who had killed particular animals. The Idoma elders had an elephant mask that was over 6 ft (1.8 m) long!

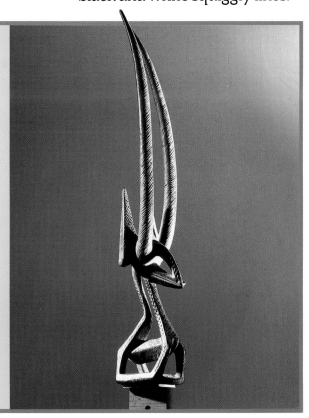

4 Fold the trunk like an accordion to make pleats. Then paint lines across the pleats to make it look like a real trunk. When the paint is dry, glue the trunk into position.

5 Copy the shape of the large ears and cut out two from gray paper. An African elephant's ears go all the way down the side of the face. Fold and glue the ears to the sides of the bag.

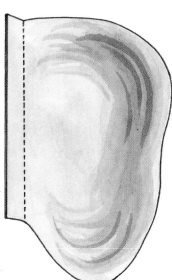

6 Cut out two pointed tusks from white cardboard. Fold them at the end and tape them on either side of the trunk.

Now you can put on your mask and stomp off like an elephant!

Halloween Frieze

YOU WILL NEED:
- ✓ large sheet of thick black paper ✓ white crayon
- ✓ colored tissue paper
- ✓ glue stick ✓ Fun Tak
- ✓ white pencil ✓ scissors
- ✓ colored foil tape

In some parts of the world, children wear costumes and ghoulish masks on Halloween.

1 Look at the Halloween frieze below and copy the shapes onto black paper with the white pencil. Add your own ghostly designs, too. Cut out all the shapes.

2 Now draw in the windows, eyes, and other details big enough so that they can be cut out easily. Carefully bend the paper slightly and cut them out.

3 On the back of the black paper, tape some colored tissue paper over the holes. Use yellow for the pumpkin's features and green for the cat's and bat's eyes

4 Glue some colored foil around the edges of the moon and stars.

5 Decorate the witch's cloak and hat with colored foil shapes, and cut some thin strips of tissue paper for her hair. Put them on with the glue stick.

History of Halloween

The Halloween festival takes place each year on October 31. It probably came from an ancient Celtic New Year festival. The Celts lived over 2,000 years ago in Britain and northern France. Their new year began on November 1. On the last day of the old year the Druids, who were the priests and teachers of the Celts, lit a huge bonfire of oak branches. The people sometimes wore costumes with animal heads and skins. Centuries later the Christian church made November 1 All Saints' Day and the previous evening became known as Halloween. Parents carve jack-o'-lanterns out of pumpkins and light them with candles. At a Halloween party you might listen to ghost stories, bob for apples, and have your fortune told.

6 Outline the eyes, mouths, wings, and claws with white crayon.

7 Now you can fasten the shapes to the inside of your window with Fun Tak.

Dough Monster

YOU WILL NEED:
✔ 2 cups of flour ✔ 2 tablespoons of cooking oil ✔ 1 cup of salt
✔ 1/2 cup of water ✔ large bowl ✔ aluminum foil ✔ cookie sheet
✔ popsicle stick ✔ fork ✔ spoon ✔ brushes ✔ poster paints ✔ varnish

1 First make the monster dough. Mix the flour and salt in a large bowl. Add the cooking oil and water to the mixture. If the mixture is too dry, add more water. If it is too wet, add more flour. Knead the mixture well with your hands.

2 Use a large lump of dough for the monster's head, and keep a small lump for extra features. Make the monster's head about 1 in (2 cm) thick. Use different objects, such as popsicle sticks, forks, and spoons to make hair and monstrous features.

3 Roll out a long dough sausage and use this to make the eyebrows and lips. Make dough balls for horns, eyes, and nose. Stick the pieces on with a little water and press them into the face.

4 When you are happy that your monster looks really horrible, ask an adult to help you bake it. Line a cookie sheet with foil and put the monster on it. Place it in the bottom of the oven and bake it for about 40 minutes at 350°F (180°C).

Grotesques and gargoyles

You can often see strange human and animal forms high up on the walls and roofs of old churches and buildings. They are usually carved in stone or wood and are called grotesques. Many act as waterspouts and are called gargoyles. To protect walls from rainwater, ancient Greek architects built terracotta or stone lion heads. A hollow channel inside the head directed the water through the lion's mouth. In the Middle Ages, architects created fantastic spouts. Many were part animal and part human. Giants and demons were popular with stonemasons, as were animals from legends, such as griffins and dragons. The only purpose of most grotesques was to add decoration and interest.

5 You can paint the monster when it has cooled. Use poster paint to give it the color of wood or stone. When the paint is dry, put the monster somewhere high up in your room. It will give your friends a fright!

Happy Face, Sad Face

1 Cut out two pieces of cardboard bigger than your face. One will be a happy face and the other will be sad.

2 Draw and cut out large holes for the eyes and mouth. Cut out pieces of cellophane and tape them over the holes with masking tape.

WARNING: Never hold cellophane right up to your face!

3 Fold a piece of cardboard and cut out a nose as shown. Stick it to the mask.

4 Tape ears to one of the masks.

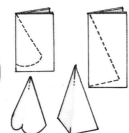

5 Paint the happy face pink and the sad face white. When the faces are dry, paint around the eyes and mouth. You can paint over the cellophane, but make sure you can still see through the eyes. Copy these pictures, or make up your own happy and sad faces.

6 Make hair for your masks. Cut strips of colored paper and roll them around a pencil. Glue the curled paper strips onto the back of the masks.

7 Tape a dowel rod firmly to the back of each mask. You can now play two different people by quickly changing masks.

Ancient Greek drama

Greek drama began with festivals held in honor of Dionysus, the god of wine. These festivals opened with a procession of singers wearing masks. Later, a chorus of singers read poetry. The poems then developed into plays. These were performed in a grassy circle, called an orchestra. The audience sat on the surrounding hillside, forming an amphitheater.

The actors wore masks that covered the whole front of the head, including the ears, with wigs attached. The masks were probably made of linen stiffened with plaster and then painted. Wearing masks meant that one actor could play two different parts, or one part could be played by two actors at different times. All female characters were played by men.

Knight's Helmet

Knights used to wear helmets on their heads to protect them during battles. These varied in shape and size.

1 Roll a piece of oak tag, about 24 x 12 in (60 x 30 cm) into a wide tube. It must be big enough to fit over your head and rest on your shoulders.

2 For the visor, cut a large slit in the helmet, $4^3/_4$ x 2 in (12 x 5 cm). Then cut strips of oak tag $1/_2$ in (1 cm) wide to fit across the slit. Tape the strips inside the helmet.

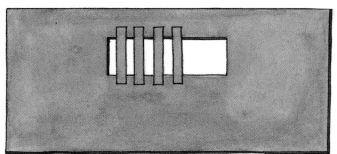

3 Paint a pattern of black dots underneath the visor.

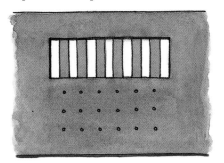

4 Try the helmet on for size. Glue and tape the edges together.

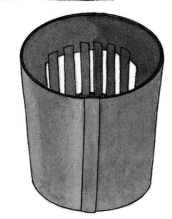

5 To make a plume, cut a wide strip of crêpe paper, 10 x 6 in (25 x 15 cm). Fold it lengthwise and cut a fringe. Wind the fringe around a straw and tape down the end. Then carefully pull the fringed strip along the straw.

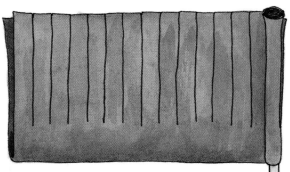
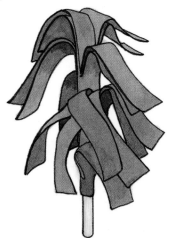

6 Tape the plume to the top of your helmet. Then put it on and get ready for battle.

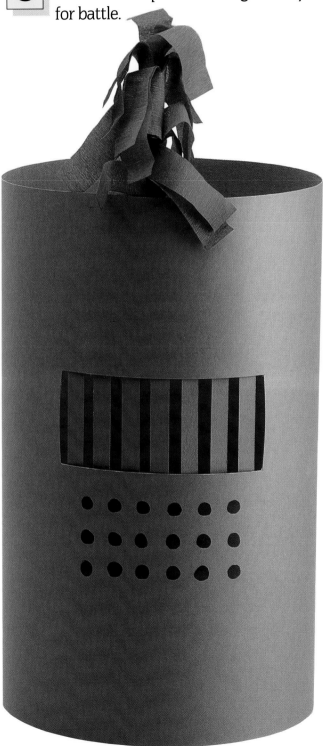

Armor

A well-armed knight in the year 1100 wore a long cloth or leather coat. Over this he wore chain-mail—a network of linked iron rings. In later years, body armor was made of strong metal plates and weighed at least 55 lb (25 kg).

On his head, a knight wore a steel helmet. Earlier types were flat-topped, later ones were rounded or pointed. After 1400, helmets came right down onto the shoulders and were fastened to the chest and back. Some had heavy visors that could be lowered to cover the face. Others were decorated with a colorful plume. Every knight had his own emblem, called a coat of arms, painted on his shield. Sometimes the coat of arms showed an animal, such as a lion, a bear, or a dragon.

Masks Around the World

People have been wearing masks for thousands of years. There are pictures of hunters wearing animal masks in prehistoric cave paintings in France.

The original masks mentioned in this book come from all over the world. You can find them on this map of the world, as well as some other countries where interesting masks have been worn.

Alaska, Canada, Greenland, Russia. The Inuit people still live in the frozen north, but most now live modern lives in modern houses.

Greenland

Alaska

Canada

Canada and U.S.A. The Haida, Tlingit, and other Indian tribes lived along the northwest coast of North America.

United States

Mexico

United States and Canada. The Iroquois Indians lived with many other tribes in the eastern woodlands area of North America. Members of their False Face Society wore frightening, twisted masks to scare off demons.

Mexico. The Aztec Indian people made skull masks inlaid with precious metals.

Peru

Where they live today:

Inuit people

Northwest coast Indians

Eastern woodland Indians

Peru. The Inca Indian people made death masks. The mummies of Inca royalty wore golden masks. Less important people had masks made of wood or clay.

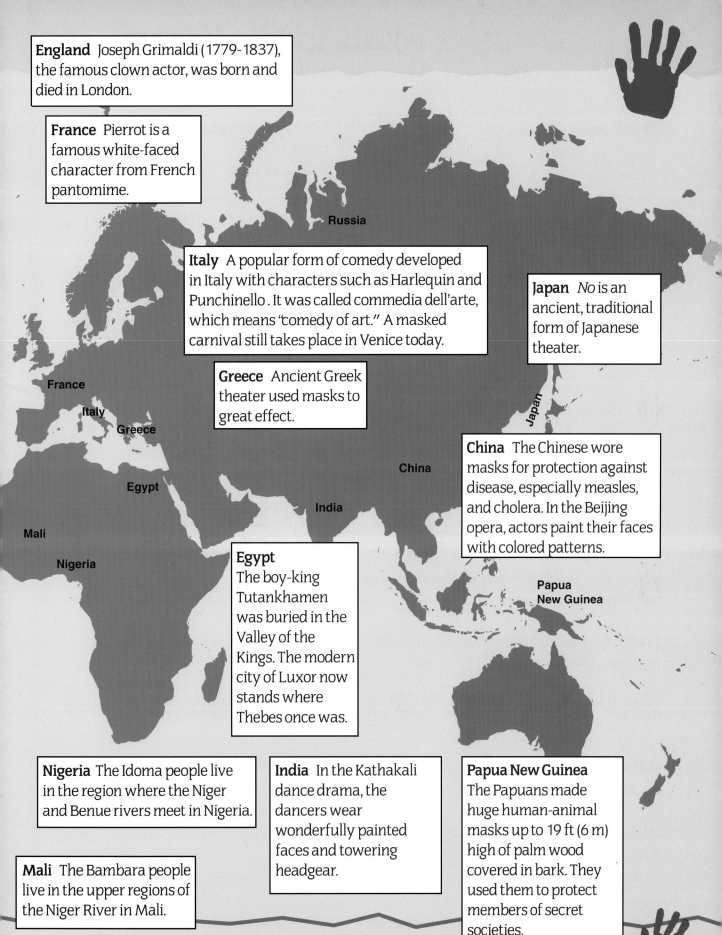

England Joseph Grimaldi (1779-1837), the famous clown actor, was born and died in London.

France Pierrot is a famous white-faced character from French pantomime.

Russia

Italy A popular form of comedy developed in Italy with characters such as Harlequin and Punchinello. It was called commedia dell'arte, which means "comedy of art." A masked carnival still takes place in Venice today.

Japan *No* is an ancient, traditional form of Japanese theater.

Greece Ancient Greek theater used masks to great effect.

France

Italy

Greece

Japan

China The Chinese wore masks for protection against disease, especially measles, and cholera. In the Beijing opera, actors paint their faces with colored patterns.

Egypt

China

India

Mali

Nigeria

Egypt The boy-king Tutankhamen was buried in the Valley of the Kings. The modern city of Luxor now stands where Thebes once was.

Papua New Guinea

Nigeria The Idoma people live in the region where the Niger and Benue rivers meet in Nigeria.

India In the Kathakali dance drama, the dancers wear wonderfully painted faces and towering headgear.

Papua New Guinea The Papuans made huge human-animal masks up to 19 ft (6 m) high of palm wood covered in bark. They used them to protect members of secret societies.

Mali The Bambara people live in the upper regions of the Niger River in Mali.

29

Glossary

amphitheater - an open, round theater, with rows of seats rising from a central arena.

auguste - a clown who wears battered clothes, colorful makeup, and pretends to be very clumsy.

Celts - a people who lived in Britain and northern France over 2,000 years ago.

chain-mail - armor made of a network of linked iron rings.

coat of arms - a knight's emblem.

Dionysus - the Greek god of wine.

Druids - priests and teachers of the Celts.

elder - a senior member of a tribe or society.

gargoyle - a waterspout in the form of a grotesque.

griffin - a winged monster with an eagle-like head and a lion's body.

grotesques - strange human and animal forms on walls and roofs of old churches and buildings.

Halloween - a festival that takes place each year on October 31.

Harlequin - a comic character from old Italian theater, who usually wears diamond-patterned tights and a black mask.

igloo - a dome-shaped Inuit house built of blocks of solid snow.

Inuit - a people of the Arctic regions of Alaska, Canada, Greenland, and Russia.

lacquer - a hard glossy coating, often put on wood.

masquerade - a party or ball to which guests wear masks and costumes.

mummy - a body preserved and prepared for burial in ancient Egypt.

No - an ancient form of Japanese theater.

orchestra - originally a grassy circle in ancient Greek theater.

pharaoh - an ancient Egyptian king.

Pierrot - a character from French pantomime with a white face, white costume, and pointed hat.

Punchinello - a mischievous character from old Italian theater, who later became known as Punch.

slapstick - comedy with lots of action and fooling around.

sod house - a house made of grass-covered earth.

Resources

terra-cotta - hard, brownish-red clay.

thunderbird - a legendary bird that produces thunder, lightning, and rain.

totem - among North American Indians, an object that represents a family.

tumbling - performing leaps and somersaults.

visor - a piece of armor fixed or hinged to a knight's helmet to protect the face, with slits for the eyes.

Books to read

Masks
by Clare Beaton
(Toronto: Warwick, 1990)

Masks
by Lyndie Wright
(New York: Franklin Watts, 1990)

Making Masks (Kids Can Do It)
by Renee Schwarz
(Toronto: Kids Can Press, 2002)

Making Masks and Crazy Faces
by Jen Green
(New York: Gloucester Press, 1992)

Native American Crafts & Skills
by David Montgomery
(Guilford, CT: The Lyons Press, 2000)

The Usborne Book of Masks (How to Make)
by Ray Gibson, Chris Chaisty, Ray Moller
(Tulsa, OK: E.D.C. Publishing, 1994)

What Can You Do with a Paper Bag?
by Judith Cressy
(San Francisco: Chronicle Books, 2001)

Places to visit/Websites

American Museum of Natural History
Central Park West at 79th Street
New York, New York 10024-5192
(212) 769-5100
Website: www.amnh.org

Brooklyn Museum
200 Eastern Parkway,
Brooklyn, NY 11238-6052
(718) 638-5000
Email: information@brooklynmuseum.org
Website: www.brooklynmuseum.org/

Cincinnati Art Museum
Art Museum Drive
Eden Park
Cincinnati, Ohio
(513) 721-2787
Email: visitorservices@cincyart.org
Website: www.cincinnatiartmuseum.org

Dallas Museum of Art
1717 North Harwood
Dallas TX 75201
(214) 922-1200
Email: jheimberg@DallasMuseumofArt.org
Website: www.dallasmuseumofart.org

Museum of New Mexico
Museum of Fine Arts
107 West Palace Avenue,
Santa Fe, NM 87501
(505) 476-5072
Website: www.mfasantafe.org

Smithsonian Institution National Museum
of African Art
950 Independence Avenue, SW
Washington, D.C. 20560
(202) 633-4600
Email: nmafaweb@si.edu
Website: www.nmafa.si.edu/index2.html

University of Chicago, Oriental Institute
1155 East 58th Street
Chicago, IL 60637
(773) 702-9520
Website: www.oi.uchicago.edu/OI/default.html

Index

Additional Photographs:

B & C Alexander 13(b); e.t. archive 25(b); Chris Fairclough ColourLibrary 21(t), 23(br); Werner Forman Archive 18(b); Robert Harding Picture Library 17(br); Japan Information and Cultural Centre, London 9(top, both);National Trust Photographic Library/Mark Fiennes 27(r); Peter Newark's Western Americana 15(t); Zefa Picture Library 7(tr) (cover).